THINGS I WISH
HE KNEW
OUR LETTERS OF TRUTH
from sons to fathers
and fathers to sons

Marc Antoine, Kelvin Lesene Jr., Keenon Mann, Marquan Newman, Perdu, Herb Middleton, Donte, Gregory Jones, Josh Minor, Akin

Introduction by

Mister "Daniel" Middleton

www.VisionDirectives.com

P.O. Box 13120/ Wilmington, DE 19850

Cover Design by Minor Design Co.
Cover Model: Jino Oguns

DEDICATION

This book is dedicated to the bold men who have taken their freedom and healing into their own hands and to those who will be inspired to do so after reading these letters.

CONTENTS

Your Letters Begin

ACKNOWLEDGMENTS

We'd like to acknowledge all of the men that have contributed to the life of these letters. Thank you for opening your heart and soul. Thank you for being transparent.

Thank you for being concerned about your healing and the healing of your sons, nephews, neighbors and fathers.

Thank you for giving hope and starting the conversation to your own healing and the healing of the next generation.

We acknowledge you today.

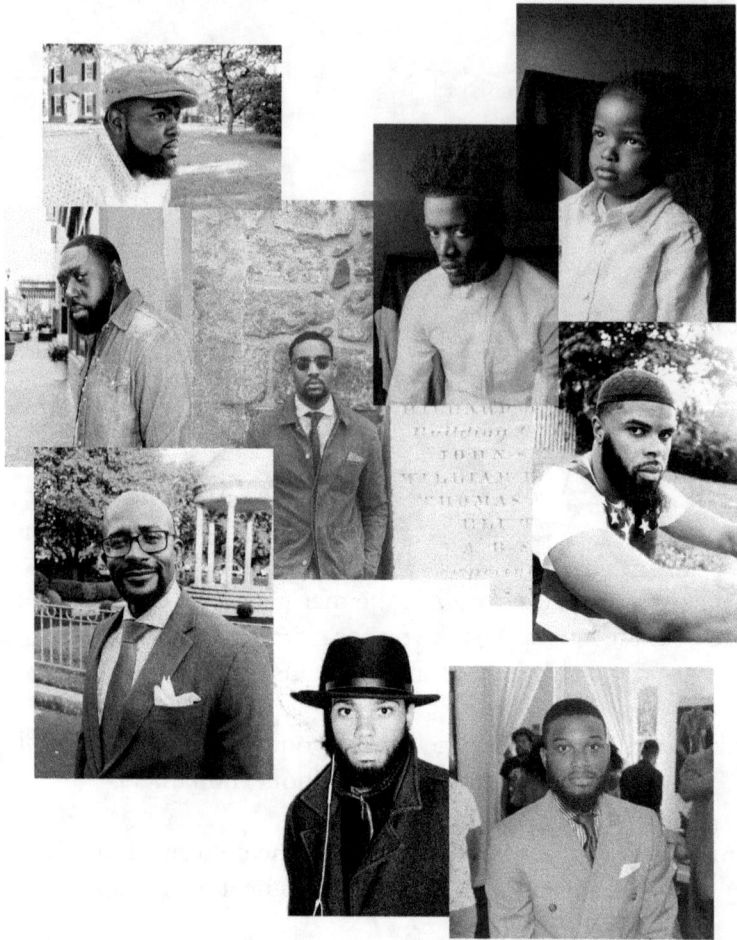

"*What was silent in the father speaks in the son, and often I found in the son the unveiled secret of the father.*"

–Friedrich Nietesche

INTRODUCTION

The "absent father" epidemic is an unfortunate, seemingly generational, occurrence. It has plagued numerous homes and families. Truth is, it has no ethnical boundaries and no demographic structure, but as an African American man I've seen how this "curse" has affected many within my community. Fathers being absent in the lives of their children appeared to be the norm. Even I was a victim of such a reality. I suffered growing up without the active presence of my biological father. Certainly, there were other men in my life I could look up to however there was still a void. For years, I harbored feelings of hurt, rejection, anger & loneliness. I had a distorted view of what fatherhood and sonship was all about.

In a message addressing fatherhood, President Barack Obama stated, "We need fathers to realize that responsibility does not end at conception. We need them to realize that what makes you a man is not the ability to have a child – it's the courage to raise one." Being a father is more than just being a male parent; it is also a responsibility. As men who have children, it's our responsibility to father our offspring. What does this mean? It means we must take action! Being the primary active figure of protection, the voice of affirmation, guidance and support in the lives of our children. The duties of a father can be challenging, but we must strive to overcome every challenge and break every cycle, which denies our children the right to a life of security.

There is a song entitled "Father Me" by Shekinah Glory Ministry. The lyrics are simple, yet powerful; "Father, wrap me in your arms and father me!" It resounds the cry of a child to be fathered, the hope of a child to be protected, the desire of a child to be affirmed, and ultimately the need of a child to be loved.

So to my son I say: You are loved. You mean the world to me. You are beautiful inside and out. Not only are you my offspring but also and ultimately, you are a child of a loving God. We share some attributes, but you were created in the image of God. You are strong. You are a leader and not a follower. You are whom God has made you. You walk and talk with confidence. I want you to know your life is valuable. Don't ever loose yourself trying to be someone you are not. I love you, always and forever.

– Signed, your Dad.

...And to my father I say: As a child, I cannot remember you being around as much as I would have wanted or needed. I remember finding contentment with the idea of "at least I know who my daddy is." I can remember feeling fulfilled with hearing from people "Boy you look just like your father!" It was the only thing I felt proud about as it relates to you because it gave me a sense of identity. As a young man entering adulthood, I've experienced your presence in a refreshing way. I began to feel your love and concern for my life. I've experienced you reposition yourself and take your place in my life as my father. I've experienced a reconnection. I want to say thank you for not giving up on me or on your responsibility as my father. You've not dotted every "I" or crossed every "T", but I love you still, always and forever. No one can take your place. I needed you then, but I am so grateful to have you now!

– Signed, your firstborn son.

To the reader: The purpose of this book is to allow men a platform to step out from the shadows of hidden unspoken words and speak directly or indirectly to their father and/or son. It may be something they've never got the chance to say, be too afraid to say or don't know how to say. I wanted to provide an opportunity for all men to shed light and give voice of praise, appreciation, hurt, disappointment, wisdom or instruction. I hope these letters speak to you

-Daniel Middleton

*"Every son quotes his father,
in words and in deeds."*

Terri Guillemets

1

I Wish My Father Knew
-MARC ANTOINE-

I remember going to basketball games in 5th grade; most of my teammates were accompanied by mothers, older brothers, or grandparents, but not me, I always walked in with my Dad! I remember a semi-final game that my team played in, I made a crucial shot late in the game and the crowd erupted. I can still see my father's reaction as he jumped in the air with excitement and pride. I wish my father knew that the other boys on the team were looking at him and wishing that their fathers were there to cheer them on.

He was there. Yes, he was a great teacher, leader, and musician, but most importantly he was there. He was a linguist and a handy man, a comedian and an athlete, a choir director and an inventor, but most importantly he was there. He did a lot for me, but each and every action pales in comparison to the essence of his presence. He was there. While his actions meant the world to me, his teaching formed my character, and his sacrifice led to my success, it was the power of his presence that had the most impact. I wish my father knew how influential our prayers together before bed were. I wish my father knew how important it was that he was at home when I got back from school. I wish my father knew how powerful it was to see him care for my mother.

I know my father knew that the kids at school made fun of his heavy Haitian accent. I know my father knew that the other kids at the park laughed at him when he tried to play basketball with us. I know my father knew that the other kids made jokes when he played the accordion during church service. But I wish my father knew that their laughs, jokes, and the teasing never mattered to me. I wish my father knew that I wasn't bothered when he came to my school, or when he came to the park, or when he played the accordion. I wish my father knew that to me, he was the coolest!

I hope that my future son will see in his father what I saw in mine. I pray that I can be as present physically, spiritually, emotionally and psychologically in the life of my son as my Father was in mine. I wish my father knew that he was the rock that was thrown in the ocean, and his ripple will never end.

"....I guess I would say to him, a dollar is nice, but I'd rather you be there.

When I was growing up, my dad wasn't always in the picture. He was there but always from a distance. He'd send money for school...for my birthday, but you know that doesn't beat actually being there.

A dollar is nice but I would've rather you been there. - Seyi A.

2

Message to My Father

-KELVIN LESENE, JR.-

I was talking with a kid that I mentor not too long ago and he shared some eye-opening things to me. We were talking about school and sports and why he was having trouble in both, his answer was; "I miss my dad. I wish my dad was in my life like the other kids I know. My friends are always talking about how they did things with their fathers. How their fathers came to their schools and did things with them on the weekend. How they came to their football games and taught them things. I wish I knew mine. I wish he loved me like my friend's fathers love them."

As I sat there in complete awe and shock, I stepped back from the conversation for a second and evaluated my own relationship with my father. I haven't spoken to my father in almost 10 years. One day he just essentially "disappeared." For me the hardest part wasn't my father not being there for me, it was watching my mom struggle to make ends meet. I always had this idea that if my father was around then we wouldn't have had to struggle. There's a preconceived notion that if you have both parents then your life is seemingly perfect. As I grew older I started to learn more about myself, God and how the world works. Gratefulness filled my heart when I realized maybe we didn't have both parents, but at least, we had one that loved us; instead of two who couldn't stand each other.

Being a child I sat around for a while, pondering the same questions that this young man was searching to answer. One day I looked in the mirror and told myself, "no matter what, I will be a great man, with or without my father in my life." I once heard a pastor say "God may not have let your father stay around because generational curses needed to be broken, and if he would have raised you, you may have come out just like him."

I in no way want this letter to be a bashing session, or even a place to vent, but what I do hope people get from this letter is to speak to the invisible man, my father. My mother told me that he see's the things I post on Facebook and that's how he keeps track of me, funny thing is, the "add" button works better than most people know.

When my dad was around he taught me what assets and liabilities were (I was 10 at the time). He taught me that assets are what people take ownership of and take pride in; what they value in a sense. I've come to realize I must not have been his best asset because he didn't take pride in me. I must have been a liability.

If you're like me and your father is not in your life, a decision has to be made, (prayerfully the sooner the better), that you'll be a better father than your father was to you. I had to come to the realization that no matter what, I will not use the absence of my father from my life as an excuse. The bible says the steps of a good man are ordered by the Lord (not the steps of a man with a "father"). Life is about choices and what makes a man are the decisions he makes and how he lives with those decisions. So today if you have no father in your life, I challenge you to make the decision to be a better man!

How long as a generation will we continue to blame not having a father on the reason why we still struggle to be men? I understand a woman cannot teach a man how to be a man, but a woman can teach him how to love a woman and that's half the battle if you ask me. Too many men do not know how to love, how to be loved and a lot of it has to do with the anger they hold towards fathers that were never there. It baffles me how we still blame fatherlessness as the reason why men in our generation continue to fall short of the mark of being a man and taking care of responsibilities. Now more than ever there are coaches, mentors, spiritual leaders that are willing to play the role as a father figure, if you have one reaching out to you, embrace them.

To be completely honest no one should have to ask or beg anyone to be a man! A man is there for his children. A man, no matter what, is a provider. We're in a sad place where we have all these self-proclaimed "men" who aren't taking care of their responsibilities as a father. Until you are a father and handle all of your responsibilities when it comes to your children you will only be a grown boy.

As men it is our duty to step up and take responsibility for our fatherless children. You did not gain what success you have without the help, influence, guidance, or teachings of someone else. Take the time to give back and influence a child. Take the time to be the difference in a child's life. So many people are consumed with being "the man" in their city, that they lose sight of the goal to be A MAN at home first.

I heard someone say, "sometimes God will not let people you think you need most in your life pour into you, because spirits, demons, fears etc, that they have, God is trying to protect you from picking them up." My father had/ has spirits he was not delivered from when he exited my life, and if he had to be separated in order for me not to grow into his bad habits, then I'll forever be grateful to God. So although my biological father was not there for a great majority of my life, I'm truly grateful that up until now I had great men placed in my life to learn from. I had father figures, pastors, deacons, doctors, and lawyers in my corner who poured into me what I needed to be successful up to this point.

I challenge every person reading this letter to help a young man find his stance. Help him find his balance. Help him to become a man of substance, of character, integrity, passion and drive. A man is firmly grounded in who he is and his purpose here on earth. No matter how different his ideas may sound, no matter how far from the norm he is as a person, he will never change his stance because he know it's a part of his destiny.

Now I pray for everyone reading this letter;

"Father in the Name of Jesus, I pray for every individual person reading this book, I pray healing, restoration and deliverance in the name of Jesus, that you rebuild what was once torn down by absent fathers, give strength where there is weakness, and protection caused by a father now being there. I pray

God that every person reading this book who may be missing a natural father, that you wrap your arms around them and show them your unconditional love. We pray God that every person who may have turned away from you God, or does not know you now see you through these pages. God we ask now that every spirit of abandonment, every spirit of rejection, every spirit of loneliness be cast down in the name of Jesus. We pray God that you send men who can be a leader in the lives of those in need of a father figure God. Send men of character, men of integrity, men of courage, men of prayer and of faith to fill that missing void. We even speak to each individual person reading this book that they have a renewed love and understanding of you. We thank you God and we bless your name. In the name of Jesus we pray, Amen."

-Kelvin Lesene Jr

"The absence of a father does not negate the need for one."

Author - jwm

3
Dad, My Life Means A lot
-AKIN-

A lot of people would look at me and say, "he's lucky, he got it, or he probably living good." The world can only see what we let them see, not everything is what you perceive. Growing up I questioned everything, so as a child I was very observant. My mind would wander, I wondered, why am I living in this condition? As an adolescent I would question, do I have a father?

Many years, a part of me felt incomplete, due to the fact I was a fatherless child. Now, many people have been in this position and have turned out to be great and some have not. Unlike some I'm glad I went through this experience of not having a father present. It instilled and molded me into the great black man I am today. Only thing that can hold you back from succeeding is yourself. We have a choice to ourselves to be great and I owe that much to myself. It wasn't an easy journey getting to the point of closing that chapter in my life. But as I got older I knew it had to be done, finding the closure that would help me grow as a man. When I share the story of my mother being raped as how I was conceived the look on people's faces...a stare of dismay facial expressions. We all have a story and this just creates the blueprint of our destiny. When I unraveled the true story of my life it was hard to bare at first, but I could finally let go and live even more. The moral of my story is don't let your situations hold you back or damage you to the point of not reaching the unlimited potential you have ahead of you. Understand the situation for what it is and grow out of it to make a change for the future.

-Akin

"Never mistreat and abuse your wife and think you can still have a relationship and a normal life with your son."

-Keith O.

4

Dad, Where are you? Oh, I See
-JOSH MINOR-

Dear Dad,

November of 2009, my mom called me and uttered words that still shake me today. "your father just called me. He wants to meet you." My WHAT? ... I was told you died years ago. I was told you were in prison. I was told you were nowhere to be found. I found myself thinking, "So where did you come from? Why did you come? What, you need a place to stay or some money? Well I don't have anything to give you, so its best to just move on." The phone rang, and it was you. I knew how I should have felt. Hurt, sad, angry, emotional; I

even tried to force myself to cry but nothing. I was just
skeptical. You have to understand though Dad, my
entire life, men have come into my life under the
pretense of being a father figure. The thing is, they
were always just that...a figure. At that point I had
been taken advantage of and abused for so long the
only person I trusted was myself and even that was
wavering. Not all were bad; my pastor and some other
men at the church really saw to my upbringing. While
with them I felt safe, solid, grounded; but I still
couldn't shake the notion that they were only a figure
of what you were supposed to be. Every night they
went home to their wives and children. Every night I
went home to an ailing mother and an emptiness on
the inside. Life had gotten really dark. I couldn't stand
to be alive anymore. It wasn't fair. What had I done to
not have my father in my life, loving me? I saw other
kids who had both parents, kids who were "bad", who
always voiced their disdain for their parents. Why did
they get to have two of them? As a child I had so many
questions that I felt I couldn't ask. I was young, but I
was mature enough to know even the smartest person
in my world (my mom) couldn't answer. I grew up
holding on to this and couldn't talk openly with them

about the real issues in my life. This is when I met the one man than would change my life forever. He was everything I needed and more. We talked about everything; school, my mom, church...my future. He had insight that I never thought was possible, I was taken on a journey to manhood that was very different than the rest. He understood me better than I understood myself. The talks we had about you led me on a path of forgiveness that set my soul free. He told me once, "know no man after the flesh, he's not who you think he is". I didn't understand at the time, but now I know what he meant. You weren't this random man who deserted me, you were a man on a mission of love. He helped me to understand that all things work together for my good. He led me to a place of peace where He was the Prince. I watched Him comfort my mom in the painful moments of raising a son by herself. He spoke words that became my reservoir of strength when I got weak. He was the public face of my private struggles. He carried me during my depression, loved me in my self harm. He became the closest mentor I had; more than a father figure, he became my Father. His name is Jesus and it was my deepest pleasure to introduce you to Him. Watching you grow as a believer was the greatest joy of my life. I saw how He changed you like He did me. I became to understand the love of my father via the love of the Father. It was beautiful to feel the years of pain and rejection between us melt away as you and I grew closer. You became such a bedrock of identity for me. Knowing who my father was, seeing you, hearing you was at times unreal.

It was a warm June day, I was at the lake with my friends, just enjoying the everdayness of life when my phone rang. It was my mom, upon answering instead of hearing "Joshua, its your mother" I was greeted by "you need to visit your Father, the doctors say he has two months to live". My world stopped. I didn't even know you were that sick. As my stomach turned I did the only thing I knew to do at the moment; I called my pastor. He watched me grow up, knew most of my struggles, and was the first person I talked to about you. We prayed that the will of God be accomplished and for my personal peace, and that was it. Although it was a five minute conversation, it lasted for me through your death and is still holding me two years later. It was the hardest thing I ever had to do, watching you lie in the hospital day after day. Ever since I have known you, I've never known you to back down from a fight; and this was no different. Even though we knew the outcome, you still fought for yourself. You fought for me. You pushed through tears, pain and stage 4 cancer every time I came. I could see you were determined to never let me see you weak. Had you picked up on the notion that you had slowly but surely become my hero? It was as if you could see my heart as you spoke, answering the questions I didn't know how to ask. Then the day came where you couldn't talk anymore. That day was worse than the day you passed. You seemed to be surviving inside some sort of in-between. I remembered how you loved to hear the Bible, so I sat and would read Romans and Ephesians but I would always start with 1 Corinthians 15:20-26 & 40-58. I just wanted to do everything I could to make your transition easy as possible. Every night when I left, I'd leave a YouTube playlist of your favorite preachers and songs. Sometimes I would just sit and look at you in silence for hours, my heart screaming everything I wanted to say. I would hold your hand and just cry thinking about the future. How was I supposed to move past this without you? You had become my best friend, and in just a few hours you would be gone and I wouldn't be able to see you again. The last time I saw you was the quietest you've ever been. It was the quietest I had ever been. I didn't have anything left to say, neither could you. I left with a feeling of wholeness.

I know your life wasn't easy. I understand that your childhood wasn't what it should have been. I understand that you loved the way you knew how, and weren't going to change. I'm not blaming you for anything, I stopped that a long time ago. I just want you to know my journey. You always talked to me about yours, but I never really opened up about mine to you until now. You didn't know the deep questions I had for you, or the real feelings I felt. I had to forgive myself for shutting you out and for beating myself up about it. You saw so much in me, and it pushed me further than I ever thought I could go. Thank you for being a father the way that I needed. Thank you for finding me and wanting to be in my life. Thank you for letting me know that love is real, but most importantly dad, thank you for reconnecting me with my Father. Reuniting with you caused me to grow deeper with Him. Just as I ministered to you, you have no idea how much you did the same for me. You taught me the importance of hearing, laying pride and ego aside, to speak up for myself when I'm being wronged, to always stand on the side of truth; no matter who it affects, and to show love to everyone around me as much as I can. I love you Dad, and I miss you everyday. I still can't believe you aren't here anymore. We shall meet again, this time both of us will be better than ever. Until next time sir.

Love Your Son,
Joshua S. Minor

" Dad,

 I am the man I am today

because of you."

-Love Alex

5

Your First Born Son
-KEENON MANN-

Dear Dad,

First of all, it feels weird calling you the D-word, because I know you've never seen or heard me use that word toward you. I'm writing you now, because for the first time in my life, I know where you are and I know you're not going anywhere anytime soon. I just celebrated my 16th birthday, and sadly I've only seen you two times (that I can remember). Even though we haven't shared many words in my life, I want to take the time to thank you for how you've molded me into the young man that I am. I'm sure you don't realize it, but you've taught me a lot!

July 18th, 1992. I'll never forget that date. The night before, I took my time looking through my closet and drawers in search of the perfect shirt, something that would show that I was a cool kid and clean, *and* athletic too. It just made sense to me. At 10 years old, those kinds of things meant a lot to me – that people think I'm cool... and clean... and I could ball. Found the shirt, the one that looked like a Sixers jersey. Aaaand I gotta have the right shorts and belt to match the shirt. The jean shorts – yeah, 'cause they pretty much go with everything. At least that's what Mom said, and she knows! Shirt, shorts, belt,... yeah, and those tube socks with the blue double-stripes that'll land right under my knees when I pull 'em all the way up (yes, Mom I put lotion on my knees!). And I already know which shoes I'm gonna wear. Duh! My high-top shell-toe white Adidas I got for my birthday. I'll just use a little bit of bleach and some cleaning spray under the kitchen sink and my old toothbrush. Gonna get them shoes RIGHT! And I will. I always do. Okay, what else?

Mom said to pack some deodorant, soap and washcloth in a little sandwich bag, my toothbrush and toothpaste (just in case), and an extra pair of underwear and t-shirt (also, just in case. you never know!). 10 o'clock...? I didn't even yawn yet and Mom's still up in the living room watching TV but I shooouuld get some rest for the morning.

So, yeah on the morning of the 18th, I got up before the sun the first time, but I could always go right back to sleep, so I did. But it didn't last long. "Ain'tchu spose ta go today?" my little brother asked, with some reserve in his voice. He really didn't like when I went somewhere without him, but I mean, he understood. "Yep, be leavin' soon too." Piece-by-piece every article of clothing and accessories and supplies and such were added on, like a Mr. Potato Head, till all ducks were in a row, all T's were crossed and all I's dotted.

"YOU READY?"

"Yes Mooommm!!" She knew I was ready hours before, but she always checked. I think she was kinda nervous too. It was a Saturday, and my boys were coming over to the house, like they did every Saturday to find out if "you and your brother can come play basketball, football, baseball, or ride bikes down the road," but I had agreed to give all that up, because you were coming to pick me up for the first time. I didn't know where we were going and didn't care, because my hero was coming to get ME, to pick me up and take me on an adventure. Once before, I had seen you at your parents' house, and I remember that you briefly talked to me in their house. Then we went outside and you scooped me up, spun me around, placed me atop your shoulders while in one move my hands left and right ran a swift relay race around your neck and those same hands boomeranged their way around your neck until fingers clasped forearms and there I was safe and secure on your back as you embarked on a bicycle-ride journey down the road, whirling and splicing through the wind with every pedal. The Summer air turned my wide-open mouth into a hot air balloon and my cap nearly leapt to its demise. But I caught it. Quick reflexes. That was the only time I remember being with you, and it was an adventure.

So, on the 18th... By the way, my birthday is on the 18th too, of April.

On the 18th, my boys came like they always did, and I remember telling him with an inflated chest, "I'm going somewhere, ... waiting for my Dad to come. I'm going with him somewhere today." So, they didn't go riding bicycles down the road to our regular hangout spot, and I knew instantly – they're lingering around my house with my little brother hoping that they'll catch a glimpse of you when you come. "You CAN'T look that much like him, because you look JUST LIKE your mom," they said, and I didn't know how to respond. I didn't really remember what you looked like. I DON'T remember what you look like. I would have, if I had seen you that day. Seconds peering around the house down the driveway at each passing car turned ever-so-slowly into minutes walking back-and-forth down the driveway glancing down the street then dragged on into hours as the sun slow-dragged across the sky tiptoeing toward the horizon again. My boys left to go home. My brother kept asking me to come in the house and play video games. My mom made sure I ate breakfast... then lunch... snacks too. Then the talk happened.

"Hey, come here Son," and this is where my visual memories become a blur. Not because I forgot, but because I had been fighting against my own 10-year-old emotions for hours. For hours telling myself a series of excuses and reasons that kept the flowing, wind-blown cape fastened about my hero's neck. I can't see Mom, but I can't avoid hearing... "Remember how last week, we made plans to go to the mall? We had the time all picked out and knew which stores we were going to and everything. Then what happened? Mom (when she got really nervous and was searching for words to say, she'd refer to herself in the 3rd person) didn't expect things to go wrong with the car and those unexpected errands I had to run, and we ended up *not* going to the mall, right?" I nodded up and down, cheeks warm and damp, eyes burning lightly. "Now, if that happened to us, I bet something like that happened with your Dad, too... Let's go in the house and have dinner. I'll find out what happened and we'll do something fun tonight, okay?" No matter how much Mom knew that you had let me down ... something within her must have recognized that I needed to think positively (or at least NOT think negatively) about you. That night, we went to the beach. It was fun. But it was not enough.

It was that day that I vowed to myself to never make

my child feel *those* emotions for *those* reasons, to never make a mother have to politic with her child to infuse in him, against all reason, some empathy and compassion for a person who was making no attempts to build a meaningful relationship with a person whose existence they (you) were responsible for. I vowed to myself that I would do everything in my power to never hurt a woman. (Mom never went into detail, but I knew by the way she told me, "Be careful with those eyes of yours. You have your dad's eyes" that somehow they were responsible for drawing her in, convincing her that you would be there... for her.) I vowed that I would graduate from high school, go to college and make something of myself so I would have something to give to my child[ren] and wife (not in that order). Somewhere deep down inside, I had a notion that I didn't have to BE the same kind of guy that you had been. I would accomplish an astonishing feat. I would be the opposite of that kind of guy. You'll never understand how long it took me to go to sleep that night. Or the unanswerable questions that belly-flopped into the still waters of my mind over and over again.

Why wouldn't he even want to see me?

Why would he tell my mom he would come then not show up? and not even call... at all. How cruel!

What had I done that made me deserve to be hurt like that?

Was I going to be just like him one day?

So, yes, I have decided that I am going to be the opposite of the kind of man that I have learned that you are, but I do want to see you. I want to know what you look like and which of my features are YOURS. I've decided that I want to come see you where you are. I don't want to say the J-word (or the P-word), but that's where you are, and I'm not sure how long you'll be there. There are a few things I want you to know about me:

I don't think you know this, but I have my step-father's last name, and I have since I was about 2 when he married my mom. He's been there for me, and most people don't even know that I'm not his biological son. No, we don't always see eye-to-eye, and I can't bring myself to call him Dad either, but he's been there since before I can remember.

I don't know if you'll read this letter or not, but I've

heard I have younger siblings. Honestly, I don't know if you and I will ever have a relationship, but at least let me know who *they* are, where they are. I would like to be in their lives and I would like them to be in mine.

I don't know how to tell you this, and I know it's awkward in a letter, but I've also heard you have cancer. I can't say that I am afraid you'll die, because sadly I don't know you, but again, I would like to meet you before... well, I want to meet you, so if you read this – I included a self-addressed envelope with this letter. If you can, write me back when you can. I won't keep my fingers crossed or hold my breath waiting, but if you do, I'll appreciate it. I don't have high hopes for us. I'm just a fan of giving people chances, even when they don't give me a chance. I have many memorable events coming up in my life – high school homecoming, prom, graduation, church plays, and a lot of other stuff. I'm not against you being a part of those. I'm okay with it, but I don't want anymore broken promises.

I'm your oldest son, and I don't know you. I'll be an adult in a couple more years, and you can't claim any responsibility for my successes. Another man has raised me and he is my father as far as everyone at school, church and our community are concerned. I can't imagine being okay with that, but maybe you are. I want you to think about what my life has been like wondering who you are, what you look like, how you think, what things you do *that I do*, and if you'll ever want to make time to learn about me.

Sincerely,
Your first-born son.
Keenon Mann

"...I've deleted him from my life pretty much as a person...and I had to step up most of the time in the home.

I think that experience gave me a lot of backbone, so he definitely aided me in my life...in a negative way I guess, but I can filter it through to something positive."

- Eric C.

*"When you teach your son,
you teach your son's son".*

The Talmud

6

Daddy Issues
-MARQUAN-

Dear Dad,

As far as I can remember way back when I was very young in the 90's I've been writing you letters. You were incarcerated from 1994 to 2005. I was 7 and when you were released I was close to turning 19. Over the years I've told you how much I missed you, how much I couldn't wait 'til you got home, I've updated you on certain things such as school and where I was in life. It was easy to say those things because these were things that I wanted you to see on paper. When things were going sour at home you were the one I could run to so to speak and crawl up in a corner, grab a pen and piece of paper and just write to you all the exciting things I was doing. As you know we lived in what they call "the hood" in a house with Moms, Great grandma who had custody of me and my siblings and Grandma who often drank. They had their flaws at times but were there for us when we needed them. My mom was the one who taught me how to write you while you were in prison. Hell, mom pretty much taught me everything I know, from ball to shaving, how to talk to girls, cook, etc... I even knew what you got locked up for. She barely kept anything from me. I wasn't one of those kids who didn't know what was going on. I was always aware that you were well known and did things out in the street that would ultimately get you imprisoned. I really think that's why I was forced to grow up so fast. Even now I find myself still chasing youth because I really didn't have a full childhood. My mother was so loyal to you even through all the ups and downs y'all had been through over the years; the arguing, the abuse and the

cheating. She truly loved you dad over every man she
had been with and every b@*#h you had been with.
She tried to convince herself that she didn't care about
you but even up 'til the day she died you were the one
she truly loved. We had 1 guy who was a father figure
and took us under his wing when you weren't there
named Greg. He was around for about 2 years. Real
good guy. But it didn't last long. And of course my
grand pop who walked out when I was 10 years old. So
as you can see I've never had a consistent male figure
in my life which is probably one of the reasons I don't
trust a lot of people today. Sometimes I'm full of
resentment because I felt like y'all only thought of self
when I was a kid. You never thought how not being
around in a positive way would affect me or my
siblings. Anyway, when you came home I was excited
because this person, my dad who I had been writing
for almost 12 years could finally see the young man I
had grown to be and I could see the guy I been writing
and catch him up on things. The real things. I had so
many questions for you but also reservations as well.
Around the time you came home in May of 2005 my
mom had been through it all and I hated seeing her
like that -the drugs and alcohol. It hurt my heart so

bad to see her so down and out. I remember leaving Jersey for a little and staying at my Mom Mom's (your mother) house in Delaware that summer and caught you up on certain things. I think we picked each other's brain each day. I knew one thing for certain, you weren't the same guy I remembered all those years ago or the careless guy full of rage that people spoke of. You appeared much more calm, much more reserved. You were my dad, live and in person. As days went by and we got more comfortable being around each other. We had more intense talks about the past. You talked more because I could never work up the nerve to ask you "THE TOUGH" questions I told you about the time when I was 16 and got jumped really bad and had a broken jaw for 6 weeks. I felt like I was all alone because mom was incarcerated herself at that time and my grandma was tending to the younger kids. I remember us talking about other family members that I hadn't met yet, your pops, early life in Philly, and a baby you almost had with some girl way before me. I'm not gon' lie little stuff like that hurt me at the time. Not that there could have been another child, but the way you said it and I now know that's the way you speak "oh there was gonna be a baby with some girl way before you". I was so irritated at the time, and young but I hid it well. I look back at that and realized that I was being a bit sensitive. Then there was a time I was waking up in the morning walking around and you said "you sneaky just like your mom", STRIKE 2....Don't ever say anything bad about moms! Then the breaking point when I knew I was ready to go back to Jersey with moms and grandma was when (and you may not remember) you called me corny for whatever reason and said "I didn't need anybody to really write me, my moms was holding me down" I was devastated! I couldn't believe someone (my father) could say anything like that to their child. That particular comment lived with me for a long time until I convinced myself that I didn't care anymore. And oh yea that was STRIKE 3. Lol, I left. Honestly I look at those things and think..." wow I was so young, 18, and everything got to me" Over the years we had times that were good and times when I couldn't stand you but you didn't know that. I was good at concealing my feelings for you after you showed me a different side of the man I had written to all these years. That made me very insecure in a way because now I have a hard time letting people in assuming they will build me up then tear me down emotionally or not appreciate me. Anyway the questions I always wanted to ask you and have always been curious about are Did you really love Mom? Why couldn't you two have worked it out when I was a child?. Do you miss her? Did you ever think of us when you were in the streets before prison? Why am I not as important as your other kids? Do you love me? Why don't I see you anymore? I ask these questions not to bash you, or to make you feel any less of a man. Not to hurt you. I know people look at this and say well "you're grown now" or "you should know the answers to these questions" but honestly I don't. There's always been this uncertainty and I'd really like to know. All in all you are the man that gave me life. And nothing can change that. We are practically twins. At this point even if you can't answer those questions for me I forgive you. I'm at a point in life where I choose to release all bad feelings against anyone. I'm a man who's discovering life and discovering interesting things about myself. I'm a man who also has flaws and imperfections. A man that's aiming to make his mark in the world and there's nothing greater than that to me. I don't wanna live my life angry, resentful and full of pride. In order to move on in life with or without you I have to forgive for my peace. In a perfect world we'd have father/son days and learn new things about each other, accept one another, and have an unconditional bond, love, and respect for one another. At the end of the day you are my dad and nothing can change that. As I grow older life teaches me all sorts of things, And I know one day I'll be a father and will teach my child right from wrong, be consistent and not guide or help him in a way that is negative. Not hide anything from him, lie to him, take anyone over him or her. But I will nurture and try to be the best dad I can be. I'm a few months shy from 30 years old and I really can't believe that 20 years later I'm still writing you letters and you live right around the corner. But hey, tomorrow's another day and the SON will STILL shine.

- MARQUAN

7

Counting Steps
-PERDU.INK-

Steps that count

Counting every step

Walks that matter

Walks that mean the world to me

Walks that allow me to explore my world

Walks that feel long and short at the same time

Why we never walked

Why we never counted our steps

Why we never explored the world

Why I never meant the world to you

Our walks were never long or short

My son knows who I am

We walk together

We walk side by side

Counting our steps

Exploring the world, together

Taking our time

My father does not know me

We do not talk

We have never walked side by side

Don't know how he looks

And he doesn't
know me

My son makes me
proud

I taught my son to
count

My son's first words
were, Thank You

My son has a huge
heart with so much
love

To bad you'll never get to meet him

He would make you smile

- Perdu.Ink

"By the time a man realizes that maybe his father was right, he usually has a son who thinks he's wrong."

-Charles Wadsworth

8

Dear Daddy,
-HERB MIDDLETON-

First, I want to tell you that I miss you very much. I wouldn't dare start this letter out asking you how you're doing because I already know that you're doing better than ever.

There are so many things I want to write to you that I never got the actual chance to say to you while you were here. But before I begin bombarding you with the things I want to say, I want to let you know that I'm a father of 8 beautiful children, including a daughter

through marriage and my goddaughter. Janelle and I
will be celebrating 23 years of marriage in October.
Can you believe that she stuck it in there with me that
long? All of the children are growing up nicely from
the youngest to the oldest. Mommy is 88 now and
such a strong women, even though she gets a little
weak at times. You have a bunch of great-
grandchildren, mostly from Crystal and Tameka and
you have 2 from Daniel, and Samantha his wife. I don't
think you got a chance to meet her. She's a beautiful
wife to Daniel and mother of their two children. Your
youngest great-grandchildren are Anna and
Nathaniel. Yes, we kept your name going Dad, along
with Daniel's grandmother Anna, who passed some
years back. I'm sure yall both are having a praise
party.

So Daddy, I'll try to make this short as I can because I
don't want to take up too much of your time. Come to
think of it, I can't remember if you were ever
concerned about how much time we spent talking one
on one when I was young man. I believe because you
never spent that much time with me while I was
growing up, it caused me to somewhat repeat the cycle

unconsciously. I do know that all of my children are important to me, but it just doesn't come as natural as it should to spend quality time with them.

Over the years I've seen fathers spending time with their children at the park or playing ball on the front lawn of their houses. It's something that I wish I had experienced with you. I am so blessed to have all of my children close by, and it sometimes seem like we're so far apart. I believe the reason that they seem so far apart from me is because I missed so many years of being involved in their lives as a father. Do you know that this is how I grew up? Did you mean to raise me that way? I remember seeing you while leaving for school and most of the time in the mornings you were sleep. You never walked me to the door or said "Herb have a blessed day in school". You never prayed with me Dad.

Through all of this I'm not writing this letter to you out of anger, but just to get closure. I have a feeling that you may have missed this experience in your own childhood. I understand and can never blame you for what you didn't know. I'm thankful that your grandson Daniel is very involved in his children's lives already. It makes me happy to see this. He's a wonderful father. I'm sure Bobby and Jaron will make great fathers too.

There are a few other things that I wish you knew.

Did you see your father mistreat and abuse women? I've always wanted to ask you this question. Because I watched you at a very young age being mean to mommy. I grew up thinking this was the way to be. I found out that it wasn't Daddy. Did you know that you were supposed to be an earthly expression of Christ's love in your and mommy's marriage? Yep. I learned that when I got much older. Daddy I wish you knew how much it would have meant to hear you say that you loved me. You never told me that, even though I know you loved me. This may be something else that you didn't receive from your father. I wish you would've taught me more things about him, especially being that I didn't get a chance to meet him. You probably didn't realize that I would pick up some of your weaknesses, huh Daddy, but I did and thank God by his grace that He is my Heavenly Father that has been fathering me since you left. Do you know how many people that I called "Pop" that I wanted to be you? But no matter how many men I called "Pop", you will never be replaced, even though I missed you being the father to me that you probably didn't know how to be. I love you Daddy and will see you one day when we'll both be loving on Our Father forever......

- Love Herb

*"A dad is a
son's first hero"*

-unknown

9

Thank You
-DONTE-

Dad,

Life isn't the same without you. October makes two years since we lost you. Venus and I are staying very close to mother. Harmony actually wants us to move in with mother, to eliminate the loneliness. Perhaps we'll buy a family house. I landed a new job a month after you passed. My salary is decent and music is generating consistent income for me. I'm trying to be a great provider for the family, the same way you were for us.

In my adolescent years we didn't talk very often and I'm not sure why. My early 20's is when we really started to grow and communicate with one another. I understand that death is a part of life, but it hurts that I lost you during the peak of our relationship. I could talk to you about anything from sports, history, finances, religion, and everyday circumstances. You were a good listener. You gave sound advice and you always made sure that I was aware of the truth.

Before the paramedics arrived, your final position was of you kneeling on the floor and the couch supported your upper body. This was an instant sign that your last few seconds were with God and were able to repent. I believe I'll see you again.

Thank you for being a great protector and provider. Thank you for being a good example of a real man, strong, honest, and noble. Thank you for remaining positive even when I was surrounded by negativity. You've given me the blueprint on how to be a great father and husband. My prayer is that I implement the things I've learned from you and exceed your legacy.

- Love Donte

"A dad is someone who wants to catch you before you fall but instead picks you up, brushes you off, and lets you try again."

-unknown

10

Broken Bond
-MEQAI HERDER-

"So are you coming dad?" I asked demandingly.

"I'm leaving the bar now, I'm around the corner." He hung up the phone abruptly. I jumped up so fast I almost lost my balance. I grabbed my bag and flew out my room and down the stars while yelling, "I'm leaving my dad is around the corner." I closed the first door and locked it to the entrance into my home and waited for him to pull up before exiting the second door that leads me outside. A cold rain was

pouring hard and I could feel the cold breeze seeping
through the cracks of the door. I sat on the step
waiting in my puffy coat he got me; it was 8 o'clock
and I was sure he was coming.

10 minutes passed...I didn't question it...

40 minutes passed...my butt became numb and my
hands started to stiffen...

1 hour passed and I can't take my eyes off
my flip phone hoping he would call...

2 more hours past and I lost hope...

I threw my phone against the door with all my
might as if I were trying to strike an opponent out to
win the baseball game. I stood up fast, breathing
intensely! I was angry, confused, and so broken. Our
bond was broken...YOU LIED TO ME I screamed
choking on my tears whipping my face roughly
because my stream of tears made my vision blurry. I
slammed my fists against the concrete ground almost
breaking my hands; I ran shoulder first into the door
as if I were a linesman attempting to sack the
quarterback. I slowly turned with my back pressing
against the wooden door and slid down to the ground

and hugged my knees to my chest becoming the turtle that crawled back into his shell for his own protection.

I was in 5th grade when this happened to me and I am a senior now in high school and still conflicted. Every f@*#^ing time I look out the window when it's pouring, I glimpse back in time to this moment as a child where my father, Baron, broke the bond we once shared. It's been hard since then finding a place where we both are congruent regarding the rebuilding of our relationship. From 5th grade till now shows the relationship between my father and I to be a one-way street.

It wasn't that my father intended to leave me; I mean he loved me...at least that's what he always told me when he could never be there, my naïve self always believed him. As a young man looking forward to college my father's past actions still effect how I lead my own life.

Let's reflect back two years prier, I was a sophomore and this was my first time going to QYLC (Quaker Youth Leadership Conference) where I was finally able to open myself up and share my story. At QYLC students gained a layer of comfortability with themselves and everyone else around them due to the safe aroma consuming the airspace. We were truly seeing ourselves truly for who were are and were growing into. A day into the conference all the students participating had gathered in an auditorium. I noticed a speaker and four interpretive actors on stage and I didn't exactly know what to expect. After we all took our seats, they introduced themselves. I sadly don't recall any of their names but the room got silent once the speaker put up her hand and asked for a moment of silence. After the silence the speaker told us to raise our hand when we felt moved and she would call on one of us to come up to the stage. A few seconds went by, the racing of my heart gained momentum while my palms also became sweaty. I suddenly threw my hand up closing my eyes wishing she'd pick me but hoping she would select another student but of course she chose me.

As I stood up and walked to the stage, I felt the crowd's eyes piercing my skin. I knew they were wondering what I could be possibly going up to say and that made me nervous. Honestly I had no idea why I raised my hand, but I knew there was something deep in my thoughts needing to be shared.

So I guarded myself well in my shell; a place very familiar to me I learned to go to when I needed protection from others. Once I got on stage I sat down facing the crowd. My skin became moist from the heat of the florescent glaring lights. My heart raced faster as the intensity built, then she asked my name.

"Meqai." I muttered nervously, but still smiling.

"How are you feeling?" she questioned. Trusting her instinct that something was wrong, she was studying me hard.

"You're up here for a reason and you have something to share so share it." she announced.

As I was about to answer she stopped me and asked...

"What animal do you most identify with and why?"

I took a deep breath and looked up towards the lights that were glaring at me and answered, "A turtle."

She leaned in curiously, eyes big encouraging me to continue. I looked past the crowd that was staring anxiously at me and explained...

Fifth grade was the year everything changed

for me. The last time I saw my father was two years before I started my fifth grade year. I decided to call him one Friday afternoon thinking after I waited a few years he would answer trying not to get overly excited to be let down again. To my surprise he answered and I eagerly asked if I could go to his home with him that night.

"I don't think it would be a problem he said to me, just call me in a few hours."

"Okay!" I said.

I excitedly thought it was a closed deal, after he hung up the phone I sprinted to my room, opened my drawers and threw my clothes in my duffle so fast I didn't have time to breath. After packing I sit to catch my breath smiling, I was going to have my wishes and prayers come true. I couldn't count how many times I've been praying to see my father again. As I thought about him I slowly laid on my back looking at the roughly blue painted ceiling in my room and the loud shaky fan.

I started thinking back to my first memories of Baron. I was nine when we first met. My father got into some serious trouble years ago and went to jail the same year I was born and got out the year I turned nine. Before I met my father I carried a photo of him I found in my kitchen drawer. In the picture he looked really young and slim. I don't remember clearly if he was at a boxing match in Vegas or just a regular gym, but I do remember repeating to myself "My dad must be so cool!" I carried that photo with me everywhere I went and had it folded up in my pocket.

The day we met was the most nerve racking but excited feeling in my heart I've experienced. We decided to meet at Dave & Busters, that place was a utopia for a kid like me, games on top of games on top of games! Walking in I was getting so antsy because up to that point all I had was that photo of him. I soon spotted him and when we got face to face, all the tears of joy I wanted to shed was disguised as an endless smile that wouldn't go away. I was finally there with him. He was tangible to me. There was nowhere else I wanted to be. Him and I rushed to play all the games while my mom, step dad and step mom stayed behind and watched. I didn't care though because I was with my father. That day was about us and no one else. As hours passed and our time that night was coming to a close, he took me to the bathroom and we both stood still looking in the mirror. I will never forget that moment I looked steadily at him and myself seeing all the strong resemblances between us. Our complexion was identical, our facial structure was the same, his cheeks were just a little fatter than mine, his hands were rough and strong. I smiled when I saw his hands because I finally understood why mine were so rough and I tend to think of him whenever someone mentions my rough hands now. I finally felt whole. That was the moment I fell in love with the bond that naturally formed that night between him and I. It was something I could never forget and never let go of.

I leaned back up smiling at my first memory with my father and I timed my call perfectly. "So are you coming dad?" I asked demandingly.

"I'm leaving the bar now. I'm around the corner." He hung up the phone quickly.

I jumped up so fast I almost lost my balance, I grabbed my bag and flew out my room and down the stars while yelling "I'm leaving my dad is around the corner." I closed the first door and locked it; that is the entrance into my home and waited for him to pull up before exiting the second door that leads me outside. A cold rain was pouring hard and I could feel the cold breeze seeping through the cracks of the door. I sat on the step waiting in my puffy coat he got me, it was 8 o'clock and I was sure he was coming.

10 minutes passed...I didn't question it...

40 minutes passed...my butt became numb and my hands began to stiffen...

1 hour passed and I can't take my eyes off my flip phone hoping he would call...

2 more hours past and I lost hope...

I throw my phone against the door with all my might as if I was trying to strike an opponent out to win the baseball game. I stood up fast breathing intensely! I was angry, confused, and so broken. Our bond was broken...YOU LIED TO ME I screamed choking on my tears whipping my face roughly because my stream of tears made my vision blurry. I slammed my fists against the concrete ground almost breaking my hands. I ran shoulder first into the door as if I was a linesman attempting to sack the quarterback. I slowly turned with my back pressing against the wooden door and slid down to the ground and hugged my knees to my chest becoming the turtle that crawled back into his shell for his own protection.

As my guard went up I started questioning God, "Why am I being troubled with so much pain?"

"I prayed, wished and hoped to see my father again and you didn't make it true for me," I yelled to the sky. "You're not real, you wouldn't be putting me through this if you were!" I felt I was only screaming at myself.

My heart went cold and my facial expression went blank. I slowly stood while picking up my phone and bag then taking a long quivery attempt of a deep breath. I wiped my face well enough for no one to notice.

I called my sister to come open the door and I rushed to my room flopping face down on my bed before she had the chance to ask what happened. That night I stopped believing in god and the quintessential bond I thought my father and I once shared...

A roaring applause rushes over me as I looked out into the crowd who now shared my past tears and pain. The speaker looked at me then turns to the

crowd while raising her hand for them to silence.
Once they did she pointed in the direction of the four
interpret actors and we all turned towards them to
watch.

They all walked to the front of the stage,
wearing the same clothing and turned to me. The first
actor in the line squatted and wrapped his arms
around his legs and rocked back and forth repeating
"dad" every 5 seconds. I remembered myself doing
this. The second actress pretended to smile
wholeheartedly and suddenly broke down into
sadness and kept repeating that sequence. I saw the
sadness in my heart. The third actor pretended to
bang on a door three times then would forcefully
breath out in frustration. He kept repeating himself. I
felt the anger I once had. The last actor started pacing
back and forth while looking at his phone nervously. I
remembered my worry. The four actors continued
doing each motion they started with for a few more
seconds as we all watched. I saw a younger me who I
no longer was, at that moment I wanted to go back in
time to tell myself you turned out alright.

As I watched I saw my own story through the light of others and I started to smile, and when they stopped I thanked them because they helped me move on. I then turned to the speaker and thanked her and the crowd of listeners because it was a painful experience I kept to myself for five years and finally found the courage to share it. After I shook the speaker's hand and stood up the crowd rose with me, giving an applause of love and thanks and what I gave back was that charming smile I once thought was lost. Knowing still that there is much work needed to fix the broken bond between my father and I, I feel more confident in myself that I have the strength to mold our relationship.

"We may not always agree, but you'll always have my ear. Thanks Dad"

- Garrison

"Being a father is a choice, staying true to fatherhood is a duty".

-J. Ambu

11

Longing For My First Born Son
-GREGORY JONES-

Dearest Matthew,

Though you live far away, you are near in me, my spirit and soul as you have been since birth.

My heart longs for you, even from your youth, to be a Dad to you as I am to my other two sons. I wish you were near to hug, listen to, speak into, see your growth on a daily basis. Be there to comfort and console, rejoice and celebrate the life God gives you everyday.

I long for you to know HIM more, the one who sits on the throne, up close and personal. To live His life more than your own, to hear His voice more than you speak, to listen to His heart and obey. As God has shared with me a long time ago, I see so vividly the evidence in you His Words that have become your life. He said and I quote:

PROPHESY FOR MATTHEW

Matthew, you are my firstborn,

My might, and the beginning of my strength

The excellency of dignity (honor)

And the excellency of power.

You have the same gifts I have

To bind up the broken hearted

And to set at liberty those who are captive

When I hear those words again and again, I see them in you as we spent time together this year. I see the passion for people, compassion to heal, leadership to lead and power to enforce.

However, there is a disconnect, a way that you have designed that takes away from His Words. The lifestyle of drinking, smoking, partying has hold on you. Though you know its devices, dangers and snares, but I wonder are you aware just how much it has you, rather than HIM having you. Deliverance is the medicine for your complete freedom so that the Words HE spoke about you are lived daily.

In the natural being your DAD is a longing in my heart, BUT knowing and seeing you LIVE HIS LIFE, HIS WORDS is exceedingly abundantly above all that I can ever ask or think. HIS life in total IS YOUR LIFE.

I LOVE YOU, HE LOVES YOU MORE

- POPS

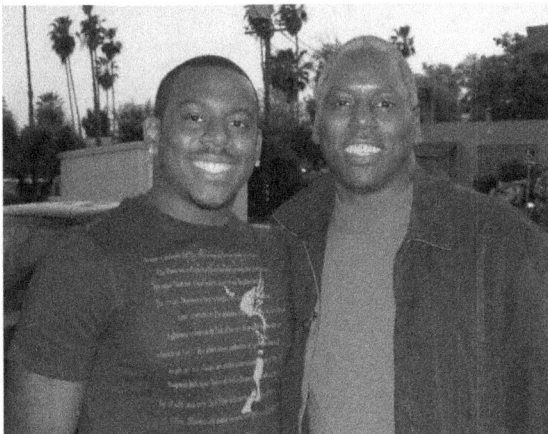

"It is not flesh and blood,
but heart which makes us fathers and sons."

- Johann Friedrich Von Schiller

"You showed me from your mistakes how to live life as a man."

\- Rashan

ABOUT THIS PROJECT

If you would like more information on any of the writers in this book, upcoming projects surrounding the book or would like to order bulk copies please feel free contact us at www.VisionDirectives.com | visiondirective@gmail.com

We know that after reading these letters you have been inspired and empowered to write your own letter. So take the liberty to write your letter right now in this book. Space is provided…go for it!!! Freedom is waiting for you!

ALSO AVAILABLE

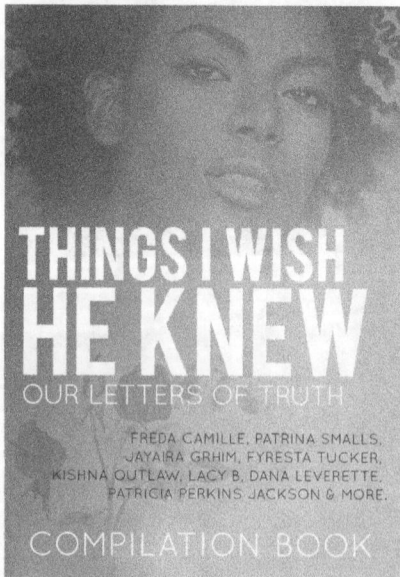

THINGS I WISH HE KNEW

OUR LETTERS OF TRUTH

FREDA CAMILLE, PATRINA SMALLS, JAYAIRA GRHIM, FYRESTA TUCKER, KISHNA OUTLAW, LACY B, DANA LEVERETTE, PATRICIA PERKINS JACKSON & MORE.

COMPILATION BOOK

Dear_____,

_____

_____

_____

_____

_____

_____

_____

_____

_____

_____

_____

_____

_____

_____

_____

_____

_____

Dear _____,

_____

_____

_____

_____

_____

_____

_____

_____

_____

_____

_____

_____

_____

_____

_____

Dear_____,

_____

_____

_____

_____

_____

_____

_____

_____

_____

_____

_____

_____

_____

_____

_____

_____

_____

Dear_____,

_____
_____
_____
_____
_____
_____
_____
_____
_____
_____
_____
_____
_____
_____
_____
_____

Dear_____,

_____

_____

_____

_____

_____

_____

_____

_____

_____

_____

_____

_____

_____

_____

_____

_____